Original title:
Rosemary Requiem

Copyright © 2025 Creative Arts Management OÜ
All rights reserved.

Author: Miriam Kensington
ISBN HARDBACK: 978-1-80566-727-8
ISBN PAPERBACK: 978-1-80566-856-5

The Solace of Fading Leaves

The leaves fall down, with grace they sway,
A dance of colors, in disarray.
They whisper tales of their old trees,
As squirrels laugh, escaping a sneeze.

In the wind's embrace, they swirl like jokes,
Tickling the branches and teasing the folks.
'We're just going south,' they chirp with a grin,
While the ground grumbles, 'Oh, where have you been?'

Dancing with the Past

In the attic's light, old photos stare,
With hairstyles bold and outfits rare.
They chuckle softly, 'What a sight!'
As shadows jive, in the pale moonlight.

Old records spin, with a creaky tune,
Reminding us of dances under the moon.
'Do the worm!' they cheer with a ghostly cheer,
While the furniture creaks, 'We're still here, dear!'

Aroma of Longing

The kitchen hums with a garlic tease,
As memories simmer, like a gentle breeze.
'Who took the last slice?' the dinner bell chimes,
While the pot eyes the fridge, plotting old crimes.

With spices swirling in a fragrant dance,
Nostalgia drifts, offering a chance.
To taste the past in each savory bite,
As we gulp down laughter, under stars so bright.

Fables of the Herbal World

In a garden of whispers, the herbs confide,
With basil and thyme holding secrets inside.
'We'll brew a potion that's silly and sweet,'
The mint interjects, with a cheeky little greet.

Sage tells a tale of a brave little sprout,
Who danced on the windowsill, ready to pout.
'When life gives you weeds,' thyme chuckles with glee,
'Just brew a few laughs, and you'll always be free!'

A Closing Chapter in Bloom

In the garden she danced with grace,
Wearing a hat way too big for her face.
The flowers giggled, they knew it was true,
She'd trip on a petal, then laugh with a hue.

With each little stumble, a story would start,
Of longing, of laughter, a humorous heart.
The daisies rolled over, the tulips did cheer,
As she recounted tales that brought everyone near.

But then came a breeze that rustled the leaves,
Tickling her fancy, as she clutched at her sleeves.
Her scarf took a flight, oh, where would it go?
She chased it through hedges, a comical show.

And as the day waned, the sun took its bow,
She waved to the blooms, "I'll visit, somehow!"
With a wink and a grin, she skipped down the lane,
A tale to remember, in sunshine and rain.

Entwined in Memory's Veil

In a garden where time stands still,
We danced with herbs and laughter's thrill.
Each sprig a note in our vaulted song,
Growing wild where we both belong.

With petals soft, we twirl and spin,
Tickling your nose, let the giggles begin.
A whisper of joy in every slight breeze,
Memory blooms 'neath the dance of the trees.

The Ghost of Herbal Remembrance

A phantom of flavor in the air,
I swear I can see you, with your messy hair.
You haunt my kitchen, pots clanking away,
As I stir up memories from our funny play.

Basil took offense at your crazy stew,
Said, "No way, buddy, that's not fit for a brew!"
We chuckled and tossed in a touch of thyme,
Yet somehow that dish should've turned into crime.

Through the Mist of Time

In the fog where our laughter collided,
The herbs of our past are forever decided.
With each little sprout, a tale unspooled,
Of afternoon feasts where jokes were ruled.

We foraged for thyme, like pirates on quests,
Avoided those thorns, like uninvited guests.
In misty memories, we giggle and grin,
Gathering moments, let the herb games begin!

A Tribute in Verdant Hues

In shades of green, we made our mark,
With pots and pans, we ignited a spark.
A tribute to laughter, a culinary jest,
Where herbs conspired to give it their best.

Parsley on plates with a wink and a nod,
Each bite a chuckle, and nothing too odd.
With minty whispers and sage on the side,
Our funny feast grows, like an herbivore tide.

Grief Beneath the Arch of Leaves

Beneath the leaves, a squirrel sighs,
Chasing ghosts of forgotten pies.
He finds a nut, it slips away,
Perhaps it'll come back another day.

The shadows dance with whimsy bright,
As laughter echoes, a silly fright.
Through trails of crumbs and playful schemes,
Death is a joke; or so it seems.

Fragrance of the Unforgotten

A whiff of thyme drifts through the air,
'Tis a tale of socks left without a pair.
Garlic breathes stories of lost galore,
Of dance-offs with garlic bread on the floor.

Phantom spices tickle the nose,
As they tango with splattered clothes.
Unseen beings, so full of cheer,
Mixing aromas that disappear.

In the Quiet of the Thicket

In thickets thick, a rabbit bakes,
Pinecone cookies for all its mates.
A meeting held with chirpy glee,
Discussing life over herbal tea.

Underneath the crooked boughs,
A frog recites its solemn vows.
"To hop for joy, to leap for fun,
Let's dance and sing until we're done."

Ceremonies of Fragmented Aromas

A funny smell wafts through the air,
At a gathering, quite rare, I swear.
With confetti made of herbs and spice,
We'll celebrate living — isn't that nice?

Jars collect whispers from every bite,
Each flavor tells a joke, pure delight.
Bringing laughter, a sweet surprise,
In fragmented scents, the memory flies.

Flowers of Regret

In the garden, weeds grow tall,
They giggle loud, they have a ball.
I planted sage, it turned to thyme,
The herbs are laughing, oh what a crime!

Sunflowers wink and daisies tease,
With every breeze, they aim to please.
Yet marigolds with stern, bright eyes,
Give me a stern look, oh such a surprise!

But in this patch of vibrant cheer,
I bury doubts, I laugh in fear.
For every bloom has tales to share,
Of tangled roots and laughs laid bare.

So here I roam among regrets,
With flower friends, no need for debts.
In this bright dance of buds and greens,
Life's simply tangled, or so it seems!

An Herb's Last Breath

Oregano sighs, it's past its prime,
Spaghetti nights, they had their time.
Basil blinks and chews some gum,
Its fragrant dreams are quite the sum.

Thyme jokes about its clumsy fate,
Forever late to the dinner plate.
Cilantro sways and starts to boast,
While parsley grins, dances the most.

The chef now melts, the dish is set,
With herbs that laugh at life's vignette.
But in this chaos, flavors blend,
Where herbs with humor, never end.

So let us toast to leafy greens,
With witty punchlines and silly scenes.
In every pot, a story stirs,
And underfoot, a dance with furs!

The Stillness Between Petals

In a vase, dreams float and twirl,
Daffodils gossip, and daisies whirl.
The quiet rose rolls its eyes,
While violets smirk, oh what a surprise!

The petals whisper, soft and sly,
A stillness found, beneath the sky.
But laughter echoes, in each bloom,
As sunbeams tickle the garden's room.

Lilies snicker at time's last chance,
While tulips prance in clumsy dance.
Each flower a jest, a playful dare,
Together they flourish, no need to care.

So here's to blooms in all their knits,
Where silence reigns but humor sits.
In every corner, joy's design,
The stillness sings, and hearts align!

Soft Chimes of Memory

The wind calls out with fragrant notes,
Lavender murmurs while basil gloats.
As memories drift like wispy smoke,
Each chime of laughter, a gentle poke.

A potpourri of days gone by,
With petals soft as a lullaby.
The herbs giggle, they share their tales,
In every spice, a ripple trails.

Chives whisper secrets, green and bright,
While rosemary's grin glimmers in light.
But each sweet chime rings loud and clear,
In the garden of life, humor is near.

So raise a toast to memories spun,
In the scent of herbs, we've only begun.
With laughter's echo, and love's embrace,
In soft chimes, we find our place!

Twilight of the Leafy Realm

In the garden of giggles, leaves spin,
The whispers of nature can make you grin.
A caterpillar wiggles with such wild flair,
While sunflowers bow with a rhythmic glare.

A frog jumps high in a leafy spree,
Chasing after shadows, as light dances free.
In this twilight hour, where laughter grows,
Even the wind joins in, just to impose.

A Symphony of Soft Scents

A symphony plays with soft scents in air,
Petunias pluck strings with fragrant flair.
Daffodils dance in a ballet of bloom,
While bees hum along, clearing all gloom.

The roses debate on who's queen of the plot,
While daisies roll dice, giving it a shot.
With petals like cupcakes, sweet to the core,
In this scented orchestra, who could ask for more?

The Fragrance of Goodbyes

The scent of nostalgia drifts on the breeze,
As leaves bid farewell with giggling ease.
A squirrel waves off, in a furry ballet,
While shadows embrace the end of the day.

A last whiff of thyme, a chuckle so light,
As crickets chirp softly, bidding goodnight.
With candles of starshine, we'll toast to the days,
For laughter and memory shall always amaze.

Dried Petals and Parting Words

Dried petals crumble like the best of jokes,
In every crease, a memory pokes.
They whisper sweet tales of a summer's jest,
Of silly adventures and frantic quest.

With parting words rolled in a paper hat,
They send off the sun with a gentle spat.
So let's raise a toast to those vibrant hues,
In laughter, we carry the scent of our shoes.

Shadows Under the Herb Boughs

In the garden where herbs sway,
The shadows dance and then delay.
A squirrel steals a sprout or two,
While we laugh at nighttime's brew.

They whisper secrets of the day,
Tales of cats who chase the ray.
Tomatoes plot to steal the show,
While basil winks and steals the glow.

The Grieving Herb Master

The master of herbs had a plant,
He cried for wilting—don't recant.
Yet every droop brought laughter near,
As neighbors quipped, "We'll drink a beer!"

With scissors poised, he made a toast,
To rosemary—his cherished ghost.
But when he pruned, he'd cut too deep,
And all his plants began to weep.

Threads of Fragrant Memories

Tangled thoughts in scents arise,
Mint remembers baking pies.
Oregano hums an old refrain,
While thyme just chuckles, feeling sane.

In the pantry lies a spice so bold,
It laughs at tales of days of old.
Cilantro snickers at the stew,
Potpourri dreams in shades of blue.

The Whispering Leaves

Leaves chatter softly on the vine,
Plotting mischief, sipping wine.
The lavender slips in a jest,
While chives play dead, it's all a fest.

"Let's prank the chef," the rosemary said,
Whisking thyme in flour, what a spread!
With laughter echoing in the night,
They dream of dishes—what a sight!

Reflections in Nature's Mirror.

In a garden where weeds do dance,
The flowers giggle at every chance.
A squirrel steals the last ripe pear,
While sunbeams tickle the morning air.

The ladybugs don their tiny hats,
As butterflies clown with playful chats.
The breeze joins in with a silly sigh,
While daisies wink at clouds up high.

Bees take turns in a buzzing race,
While ants march on with little grace.
Nature's mirror reflects our glee,
In petals' laughter, wild and free.

So let us laugh as the day unfolds,
In green adventures, nature holds.
With humor found in each flower's bloom,
We find delight in life's own room.

Whispers of an Herbal Elegy

In ghostly gardens where herbs do sigh,
Thyme and basil chat, oh my!
Parsley shares tales of veggie fame,
While sage pretends to play the game.

The garlic bulb breaks into a laugh,
Telling corny jokes on a leafy path.
Oregano whispers sweetly bold,
Of spices and secrets, stories untold.

Chives giggle at a rude ol' weed,
As laughter bubbles in herbal creed.
Each sprout among us wears a grin,
In this silly dressing, we all begin.

So join the dance of the fragrant kin,
Where humor and herbs together spin.
In nature's laughter, we find our song,
In tales of greens, we all belong.

The Scent of Sorrow

Petals weep as the wind takes flight,
While daisies giggle at shadows of night.
A fragrance lingers, bittersweet,
As flowers humor the world's loud beat.

Ferns wear frowns but only for show,
The sun bursts through with golden glow.
Lilies laugh at the clouds above,
In a play of sorrow mixed with love.

The violets hum as they sway and sway,
Tickled by breezes that come out to play.
A hint of sadness drips from the dew,
As blossoms chuckle at life's crazy view.

So scent the sorrow in sweet delight,
Where laughter dances in day and night.
Among the blooms, we find our cheer,
In every tear, a joke is near.

Beneath the Fading Fragrance

Beneath the blooms, where laughter spills,
A gratitude joyfully fills the hills.
The roses gossip in shades of pink,
While lilacs play music, oh, just think!

The lilting aroma of thyme takes flight,
Whispering stories of pure delight.
Jasmine giggles with a cheeky flair,
As honeysuckle pranks in the morning air.

Petunias boast of their vibrant hue,
While marigolds dance with a playful crew.
In fragrant realms, the silly reign,
As nature's humor drives us insane.

So join the quest for joy in the smell,
Where fading notes of laughter swell.
In blossoms light, we find the chance,
To dance with life in a merry trance.

The Weight of Wilted Leaves

In the garden where dreams go to flop,
Petunias gossip while snapdragons stop.
The daisies are slumped, their faces all frown,
While the roses roll by, laughing in brown.

A snail struts by, quite proud of his shell,
Thinking he's winning at life, what a swell!
But the weeds are plotting a nefarious scheme,
To dethrone all the bloom with their unruly dream.

The sun takes a peek, just a glint in the sky,
And the orchids all whisper, "Oh my, oh my!"
Everything wilts in the mid-afternoon,
Except for the cactuses, humming a tune.

So here in the dirt, we all shake our heads,
Laughing for joy as we lay on our beds.
With petals like giggles and roots full of cheer,
The weight of the wilted just tickles our ear.

In Shadows of the Greenhouse

Beneath the glass dome where secrets reside,
The ferns throw a party, and moss is the guide.
In the shadows, a spider attempted a dance,
But his two left legs left him without a chance.

The tomatoes are blushing, so ripe and so bold,
While radishes grumble of feeling too old.
A pepper slipped out, trying hard to be sly,
But tripped on a leaf and no one could deny.

The fans spin around, a soft breeze in the mix,
And orchids exchange their best gossiping tricks.
"Did you hear about tulip's unfortunate fall?
She took quite a plunge, but she'll bounce back next fall!"

With laughter like sunlight, we dance in our gloom,
In a greenhouse where humor and plants gently bloom.
The shadows may worry, but here we all thrive,
With every good chuckle, we feel so alive.

The Harvest of Heartache

In the orchard of wishes where apples still pine,
A pear cracked a joke that was totally fine.
But peaches were pouting, their whispers so sweet,
They're not quite as juicy, but still feel complete.

Cherries debated who's ripe for the picking,
While the plums, in the shade, were just charmingly kicking.
An apricot sighed, "I'm a bit out of touch,"
As figs rolled their eyes—this was all way too much.

When the harvest comes, we'll pretend it's a game,
Where the squishy bad fruit can take all the blame.
"Let's bake up some pies!" cried the elder with glee,
While the nuts all just murmured, "We're not part of this spree!"

So gather your heartaches, let's turn them around,
In the bushels of laughter, a cure can be found.
With sass in our baskets and smiles on our lips,
We'll feast on these follies with laughter in sips.

In the Quiet of Scented Prowl

In the scents of the night, a mystery brews,
Where lavender giggles, and chamomile snooze.
The rosemary whispers, "Don't take it too far,"
As the mint steals a chance to stretch under the stars.

Old thyme stands guard, with a wise aplomb,
While the basil gets cheeky, in this fragrant calm.
The dill tries to dance, but keeps losing the beat,
And the sage rolls its eyes at the whole clumsy feat.

They discuss all the herbs that come out at dusk,
While a clove hums softly, smelling of musk.
The laughter of thyme tickles daisies awake,
As the moonlight invites them to join in the shake.

So wander the garden, let whimsy abound,
In the quiet of nights where sweet scents can be found.
With each playful whiff, let your troubles disperse,
In a world full of giggles, life's never a curse.

The Path of Faded Leaves

Leaves crunch beneath my feet,
Squirrels giggle, feeling neat.
Whispers echo in the air,
Did I just trip on a scare?

Wandering down this silly lane,
Rabbits bounce, they dance in vain.
Every twist brings chuckles bright,
Nature's joke, a pure delight.

Crisp air tickles my nose funny,
Where's the gold? Just dust like honey.
As I stroll with cushy feet,
Life's a riot, can't be beat!

Those faded leaves, a comic play,
Cracking jokes in a bright array.
The fall, a jest, for all to see,
In laughing tones, we roam so free.

Threads of Melancholy

A stitch in time, is that a yarn?
Doodling tales of woe and charm.
Knitting smiles with tangled threads,
Who knew sorrow spun sweet spreads?

Mismatched socks, what a sight!
Dancing lopsided, day and night.
Frogs in hats croak out their wails,
While spoons declare their funny tales.

The fabric of life's a patchwork quilt,
Cuddles sewn with laughter built.
Each tear's a laugh, a quirky twist,
In sadness, joy insists we persist.

So here's to threads that make us grin,
Silly knots where we begin.
Laughter hangs, a woven spree,
In the world's craziest tapestry.

In the Shade of the Herb Garden

Basil and parsley share a joke,
Thyme giggles, then starts to poke.
In this haven of green delight,
Worms are dancing through the night.

Sage whispers sweet nothings here,
With mint strumming a tune so clear.
Their spicy banter all around,
Who knew herbs could make such sound?

Lettuce laughs with a crunchy cheer,
While carrots play hide-and-seek near.
In every corner, a comical scene,
Nature's giggles sprouting green.

Here we gather, shade from the sun,
Herbaceous charm, oh what fun!
In laughter's grasp, we find our peace,
Where silly dreams will never cease.

When the Moonlight Weeps

The moon spills tears like silly glue,
Stars blink back, 'What's wrong with you?'
A glowing face, so round and bright,
Crying jokes in the quiet night.

Clouds wear masks, they dance with glee,
While crickets croon a symphony.
In shadowed laughter, tales unfold,
Night's humor sparkles, pure and bold.

As the night wears its playful hat,
Owls hoot a chuckle, fancy that!
The world's a stage of glowing beams,
Where laughter mingles with our dreams.

So when the moonlight starts to weep,
Know it's laughter disguised to keep.
In every droplet from above,
Find the joy that twinkles with love.

The Green Shade of Farewell

In the garden where she lay,
Grass tickled her feet so gay,
With a chuckle and a sigh,
She said, "I'm not saying goodbye!"

Her hat was huge, too big to wear,
With flowers sprouting everywhere,
As bees buzzed in a silly dance,
She tripped, and took a fateful chance!

Leaves like confetti fell around,
Her laughter echoed, such a sound!
In this green shade, she might just frown,
But the daisies won't let her down!

So here's a toast, with tea and cake,
To the one who loved a good mistake,
In every giggle, lies a tale,
Of silly antics that prevail!

Reminders in Aromatic Remains

Thyme and sage, oh what a blend,
Each herb a memory, a fragrant friend,
'Don't forget your shopping list,' she'd say,
But left behind was her bouquet!

In a jar of spices, she found her fate,
With a pinch of humor, she'd never wait,
Cinnamon laughter filled the air,
As garlic dreams began to flare!

She tossed in some chives, gave a wink,
"Who knew herbs could make you think?"
The basil chuckled, the parsley sighed,
For in this chaos, joy would collide!

A sprinkle here, a dash of zest,
Each memory seasoned, truly blessed,
In the garden of scents, she'd forever stay,
Reminding us all not to lose our way!

The Garden's Final Soliloquy

The daisies danced with wild delight,
Their giggles ringing through the night,
The old oak tree rolled its eyes with glee,
"Not my turn to talk, I'll let it be!"

Sunflowers strutted, wearing their crowns,
While lilacs laughed in their purple gowns,
In this grand soliloquy so absurd,
Each bloom had a tale, a quirky word!

Petunias whispered, "Remember the bee?"
As they shared stories of 'who's got the flea,'
In a riot of colors, they cheered with flair,
For the last curtain call, they'd be quite a pair!

Then came the rain, with a twisty grin,
"I'll wash away all your past sins,
But not your fun, oh no, not that!
Keep laughing, my friends, where you're at!"

Mourning in the Meadow

In a meadow where the sunflowers weep,
A gathering of critters, secrets to keep,
"Who's got the snacks?" croaked a wise old crow,
"Grab the chips, it's a wonderful show!"

Butterflies fluttered, all decked in lace,
Feeling the grip of this somber place,
With giggles escaping like bubbles in air,
They celebrated life, without any care!

A rabbit juggled some apples around,
While the chipmunks fell over, laughing sound,
"Today we mourn, but let's make it fun,
For in every ending, there's still some sun!"

So raise your cups with a clink and cheer,
To memories shared, let's persevere,
For even in sadness, a smile appears,
In this meadow of laughter, we conquer our fears!

Lament of the Herbalist's Heart

In a garden full of green,
I lost my thyme, oh what a scene.
Basil whispered in my ear,
"Don't you fret; your heart's still here!"

Dill and chives conspired too,
To brew a potion just for you.
But when I reached, oh what a mess,
I brewed my way to herbal stress!

Sage said, "Calm, let's take it slow,"
As we danced with all the flow.
But then the rosemary bit my toe,
Herbs can be so rude, you know!

I laughed and cried, a bittersweet blend,
With parsley, my mischievous friend.
In herbal chaos, joy's no lie,
Life's a salad, just give it a try!

Dusk's Bitter Memory

The sun slipped low, day turned to dusk,
I thought of garlic; it's just my husk.
A clove too strong to suit my taste,
But at least it's better than a cake too laced!

Minty thoughts muddled in my head,
Chasing shadows like a cat, I fled.
With each flicker of twilight's glow,
A laugh escaped, a silly show!

Cilantro's scent made noses scrunch,
As oregano joined our laughter bunch.
We danced amid the fading light,
Mixing flavors till it felt just right.

Though day was done, we grinned in glee,
Embracing the dusk, oh so free.
Memory lingers with a hint of zest,
In this garden adventure, we are blessed!

The Essence of What Remains

Once I chased a sprig of cheer,
It slipped away, oh dear, oh dear.
Chives and sage, they held my hand,
Together, we devised a grand plan!

But as the hours whisked on past,
My essence faded, not meant to last.
Cinnamon laughed, "You can't hold tight,
To fleeting dreams or herbs at night!"

A pinch of humor, a dash of fun,
With thyme and laughter, we'd become one.
Yet life's a brew, a crazy mix,
Where sage and rosemary play their tricks!

In the pot of what's left behind,
A fragrant blend of heart and mind.
So I'll raise a glass to what remains,
Life's quirks and herbs, in joy, not pains!

Petals on a Grief-Strewn Path

Petals fell like tears from trees,
Joining laughter in the evening breeze.
Chasing sorrow, I found delight,
With herbs that danced into the night.

Lavender giggled, "Come, let's play,"
As we wandered without a way.
With every step, the world seemed bright,
Even sad paths can feel just right.

Minty revivals, steeped in joy,
Turning frowns like a playful toy.
"Let's spice it up," the chives they cheer,
With herbs, we sprinkle away the drear!

As petals scatter, memories stay,
In this funny life, we find our way.
For on this path, we're never alone,
With laughter's scent, we'll make it home!

Timeless Whispers

In tangled tales of ancient lore,
The herbs once danced, now they snore.
With ghosts that giggle, bump on the ground,
In laughter's shadow, secrets abound.

From kitchen to grave, a spice-filled cheer,
We stir the pot, it's all quite dear.
Who knew the sage had such a knack?
Whispers and chuckles, we won't look back.

Time ticks lightly, in slippers it strolls,
With every twist, it jests and trolls.
The cast of spices takes the stage,
For here they prove, though life may age.

In comical chaos, they make their stand,
Herbs in hand, they form a band.
From thyme to chives, their stand-up is great,
In this fragrant realm, we celebrate fate.

The Haunting of the Sage

In a kitchen where shadows do prance,
A ghostly sage gives cooking a chance.
With pots and pans, they clamor and clang,
Cooking up tricks, with an ethereal twang.

"Who needs a chef?" they playfully say,
"When I can whisk in my own ghostly way!"
Their spells mix laughter with every bite,
Dishing out joy in the pale moonlight.

With sprigs of laughter tucked in their shroud,
The dining room erupts, laughter too loud.
A dinner party that's one for the books,
With flavors so funny, and spiced ghostly looks.

So here's to the sage, a ghostly delight,
Bringing smiles and giggles, both day and night.
In culinary haunt that's quite a surprise,
Eat up, dear friends, for laughter's the prize!

In the Embrace of Dried Petals

In piles of petals, a jester resides,
With laughter like sunshine, the fragrance abides.
Each crumble a chuckle, each flake a glee,
Who knew herbs could be so carefree?

With a wink and a nudge, they float through the air,
Whispers of mischief, laughter to share.
In herbal embrace, we find joy in the dust,
Reviving the past, the absurd we trust.

Dried flowers giggle, and petals play tag,
Creating a ruckus in every old bag.
In this bouquet of giggles, we find sweet delight,
Swirling in memories that sparkle at night.

So gather ye petals, let laughter unspool,
For in the dried aromatics, we break every rule.
Together we dance in this fragrant refrain,
In joy and in jest, there's nothing mundane.

A Eulogy for the Unseen

To the herbs we forgot, we raise a toast,
In the realm of memories, they linger the most.
In laughter we gather, their essence alive,
For even in silence, their spirits will thrive.

What's this? A slip of thyme on the floor?
Slips into a pun, then tumbles for more.
"Do not weep for the lost," they jest with a grin,
"We're seasoning life, so let's dig in!"

In unison, spices start a loud cheer,
From dill to cilantro, they have no fear.
Cackles and clinks, as we toast the unseen,
With every bouquet, they dance in between.

So here's to the herbs, and the laughter they bring,
A eulogy filled with joy, let us sing.
For spices may vanish, yet stories remain,
In each hearty chuckle, they live once again.

Whispers of an Herbal Ghost

In the garden, herbs do talk,
One claims it knows how to walk.
It rustles leaves with such flair,
Then giggles, vanishes in air.

Sage makes jokes, so wise and sly,
While thyme and basil start to fly.
They dance around, what a sight!
The herbs have more fun than the night.

Parsley puns about the stew,
Crying out, 'Please, don't add the rue!'
Oregano then rolls on the ground,
Squealing, 'I'm so herbivorously bound!'

But watch your step, oh sneaky sprig,
Lest you trip on a dancing twig.
For in this patch, laughter blooms,
With herbal ghosts in leafy rooms.

In the Garden of Shadows

In shadows deep where sun won't peek,
Tomatoes gather, planning their sneak!
They chuckle softly, in the dirt,
'No veggies here, we're wearing shirts!'

Zucchinis plot to take a stroll,
Whispering truths, they've lost their soul.
As radishes roll their eyes in glee,
'Ripe and ready, let's just be free!'

Carrots grinning with tops held high,
Dare the beets, so bold, to fly.
They jump around, it's quite the show,
In this garden, friendships grow.

Mischief brews in every pot,
Lettuce laughs, but turns to rot.
Yet in the gloom, all is bright,
In these shadows, pure delight.

Memories in Dried Petals

Petals crisp from summer's heat,
Snack for mice, what a treat!
Once so bold in colors bright,
Now they're whispers of the night.

Memories flutter, soft and light,
Reminding us of wild delight.
Lilacs telling tales quite grand,
Of days spent in a sunlit land.

They chat of bees and sunny days,
How they danced in golden rays.
But now they're just a faded hue,
With stories older than the dew.

Yet dried petals laugh and prance,
In the wind, they take their chance.
For even in this calmer state,
They find a way to celebrate.

A Symphony of Dusk

As dusk descends and shadows blend,
The world begins to twist and bend.
Crickets tune their tiny strings,
While frogs prepare to do their flings.

Night blooms softly in the sky,
Gossiping stars that wink and sigh.
A breeze hums through the willow trees,
And mushrooms giggle, 'Oh, let's please!'

Bats flap by in costumes grand,
Dancing on the edge of a band.
While fireflies flicker applause,
For the artists without a pause.

As laughter echoes through the dark,
The moon leans in to give a spark.
For in this twilight, fun will last,
In symphonies both sweet and fast.

A Forlorn Bouquet

A wilting bunch finds humor rare,
With petals drooping, in disrepair.
"Why so sad?" they whisper in glee,
"We're just in style, in the land of tea!"

The stems are crooked, one quite bent,
Yet they still smell fresh—what a scent!
In the vase, they gossip and tease,
"You think we're sad? Just look at these!"

A bloom went red, the other went blue,
"I'm wilted, but nobody knew!"
They chuckle softly, passing the blame,
In this silly game, they relish their fame.

So here's to those who fade away,
With laughter to guide them, come what may.
They dance in the dark, in humor they bask,
For a bouquet forlorn is a mighty fine task!

The Wail of the Willow

The willow weeps, oh what a sight,
With branches flailing in the night.
"Cry for me, dear leaves," it said with a smile,
"I'm just practicing my drama style!"

A squirrel paused, with a puzzled frown,
"Is that a tree or a clown in a gown?"
The branches shook, a laugh did unfold,
As a breeze blew whispers of secrets untold.

The roots chuckled deep, they knew the truth,
The willow's wail was just sleight of tooth.
"I'm not really sad, just playing a part,
Life's a big joke—let's give it a heart!"

So dance, dear leaves, let your spirits soar,
For even the willow knows how to roar.
In laughter and sorrow, we find our way,
Twirling through life, come what may!

Fragrant Ghosts

Through the garden, spirits glide,
With floral scents they take pride.
"Boo!" they whisper, causing a fright,
While chuckling, they vanish from sight.

A lavender laugh, a basil snicker,
These ghosts of herbs could not be slicker.
They float and swirl with fragrant ease,
Leaving behind a tickled breeze.

"Watch out!" said thyme, "a haunting's near,
Or is it just my old friend's beer?"
And with that, they burst into giggles,
Sending through the air some chuckling wiggles.

So here's to the ghosts who jest and dance,
In echoing laughter, they take their stance.
Among the petals, they find their way,
A fragrant prank on a sunny day!

Mourning in the Herbarium

In the herbarium, a tale unfolds,
Of dried-up plants with secrets untold.
"I once was fresh!" cried the rosemary,
"Why did I end up here, so contrary?"

A sage chimed in, with a sage-like grin,
"Why worry, my friend? You still can win!
A sprinkle on pasta and you're a delight,
Just wait for the chef's spotlight tonight!"

The thyme rolled its eyes, impatiently missed,
"I'm tired of being an herbalist's twist!
Can't we just be? Just lounge and rest?
Why do we have to always be dressed?"

But laughter erupted, and joy filled the air,
In the midst of the mourners, a comical flair.
Though dried and pressed, they danced in their jars,
In the herbarium's heart, they counted their stars!

Shadows in the Herbal Grove

In shadows where the herbs take flight,
The critters dance and tease the night.
A rabbit prances with a sly grin,
Chasing scents where the fun begins.

A sagebrush whispers to the thyme,
"Let's have a laugh, it's garden prime!"
The chives chuckle, the basil twirls,
In this herbal jig, the joy unfurls.

But shh! The mint plots with a wink,
To tickle the nose when you stop to think.
With every sniff, a joke they share,
In their leafy realm, no room for care.

So linger here, and let them play,
In shadows bright, where herbs ballet.
With greens so zany, life's a thrill,
In the herbal groove, we've time to kill.

The Lost Melody of Fragrance

A lilac sang a tune so sweet,
While daisies danced on nimble feet.
But oh, the roses took a nap,
And missed the show — they made a gap!

The violets whispered, "What a shame!"
"Let's blame the sun; it stole the fame."
The evening breeze blew laughter wide,
As scent and giggles tangled inside.

A daffodil suggested a jest,
"Let's have a laugh; it's for the best!"
With pollen jokes and nectar puns,
They filled the night with cheeky runs.

And when the roses woke for light,
They found a party quite a sight.
With fragrance lost, but joy so near,
The garden played its tune with cheer.

Veins of the Earth's Heart

In the soil where wild roots play,
The earth's heartbeat starts to sway.
A worm in top hat, oh what a sight,
Danced with glee, from morning till night.

The daisies formed a daring crew,
Plotting jokes with the caps and dew.
The thyme in sunglasses had a dream,
To rule the garden with giggles and cream.

"What's this? A rock?" cried the jolly sage,
"Let's tickle it—oh, what a stage!"
With laughter rolling through every vein,
The earth's heart pulsed, alive with gain.

So, join the party below the ground,
Where funny fables and roots abound.
In the earth, where tickles start,
The veins pulse loud, the garden's heart.

When the Garden Weeps

When the garden weeps, it's not from dread,
But chuckles bottled up in their head.
A sunflower rolled a tearful pry,
"Is that a raindrop or a giggle, I cry?"

The lily pads played with splashes of glee,
Each droplet a joke from the water's spree.
"Come dance!" they called to the flowers above,
"Let's turn these tears into laughter and love!"

As the marigolds joined in with flair,
The tears flowed free in the sun-kissed air.
"Why do we fret when we can bloom?"
And with each laugh, they filled the room.

So when the garden starts to weep,
Know it's joy spilling, a secret to keep.
With every droplet, a chuckle grows,
In the garden where laughter glows.

Harmonies of Broken Stem

In a garden full of weeds, they sing,
The flowers laugh at everything.
A bud with charm, a leaf on the run,
Frame a dance, oh what fun!

With petals flying, a whimsical show,
Dancing with rabbits who nibble and grow.
They jest about roots, tangled in fate,
Stepping on thorns, never too late.

The wind joins in, with a giggle or two,
As blossoms whisper, what next shall we do?
A pot on the stove, herbs wilt in despair,
Chasing a butterfly, oh, life is fair!

Yet watch where you step, on the ground - beware!
For the tiniest thorns are lurking down there.
In laughter we stay, from dusk until dawn,
While a squirrel prances, just flaunting its yawn.

A Hearth of Herbed Heartache

In the kitchen, a pot bubbles bright,
With herbs discussing their culinary plight.
The basil dreams of being a star,
While parsley scoffs, 'You won't go that far!'

A pinch of sorrow, a dash of delight,
Carrots chuckle, and onions take flight.
'The more you cry, the sweeter we stew,'
Said the garlic, whose wisdom always rings true.

Dancing with olive oil, they swirl and glide,
Making mischief from the pantry's wide side.
But beware of the clove, it can't take a jest,
With tears in the pot, it believes it's the best!

As the oven hums, an audience of spice,
The air fills with laughter, oh, isn't this nice?
In this hearth, a blend of smiles and sighs,
Herbs savor the chaos, with twinkling eyes.

Elysian Respite Among Thorns

Nestled between roses, the daisies convene,
With gossip and giggles, a light-hearted scene.
They plot how to trick all the bees on their quests,
Declaring, 'Dear friends, we're the true floral guests!'

The thorns have it rough, all pricking and prickly,
While violets joke, their tones ever sickly.
'Let's throw a gala, invite the whole field,
And dance with the weeds, oh, what joy they'll yield!'

A butterfly flutters, quite lost in the shroud,
Wings shimmering brightly, feeling too proud.
Yet tangled with stems, it trips and it spins,
And the daisies laugh, playing childish chins!

While the sun dips low, casting shadows and fun,
The garden keeps laughing until day is done.
Among thorns and petals, they'll thirst for some cheer,
Joy springs eternal, and humor is here.

Shadows of Fragrant Farewell

Under twilight's glow, the scents start to twine,
A farewell so sweet, like a glass of fine wine.
The lavender whispers a lullaby low,
While the thyme rolls its eyes, 'It's my show, don't you know?'

Daisies bid adieu, with a perky good night,
As tulips complain that their colors aren't right.
A sage with a smirk, proposes a toast,
'Here's to the herbs that we love the most!'

The breeze carries laughter, a fellowship warm,
But rosemary snickers, creating a charm.
'This party's quite fragrant, but space is so tight,'
The herbs shove and shuffle, in comical plight!

As darkness envelops the garden parade,
With humor in shadows, their memories made.
Though farewells are bittersweet, they giggle and cheer,
For laughter, my friends, is always sincere.

A Garden of Forgotten Dreams

In the garden where weeds take a stand,
Gnomes dance awkwardly, not quite planned.
Sunflowers gossip, they twist and sway,
While daisies play poker, what a funny fray!

Bumblebees buzz with a comedic spin,
Telling bad jokes, it's a real win.
A fickle wind tosses petals around,
While the garden gnome wonders, 'Where's my crown?'

Rabbits in waistcoats peek from the grass,
Critiquing the flowers as they awkwardly pass.
'Is that your hair, or did you just bloom?'
Laughter echoes beneath the bright moon.

In this patch of green, where silliness grows,
Even the cacti wear colorful clothes.
Forgotten dreams dance with frogs on a log,
In a garden of laughter, quite a fun cog!

Shadows of the Withered Sprig

In the shadows where laughter used to ring,
A wilted sprig thinks it's the next big thing.
'This old bark is a talent,' it boasts with glee,
While squirrels roll their eyes, 'Oh, let it be!'

Clouds poke fun, in a drizzle they play,
Mocking the sprig on its forgetful day.
Leaves that once whispered now gossip behind,
The tales of the crumble, oh, aren't they unkind?

A shadow-box dance with a ghost of a bloom,
Twisting and turning, it fills up the room.
'I'll sprout more life if you just wait and see!'
Cries the hopeful sprig, oh, where's the decree?

But nature just giggles, and carries on bright,
As the sun casts its shadows, a funny sight.
While the sprig dreams of glory in the fading light,
The garden keeps laughing, oh, what a delight!

Echoes in a Silent Grove

In a grove where whispers dare not tread,
Echoes of giggles swirl in the overhead.
Trees throw their branches in comical flair,
While grasshoppers hop with debonair air.

A lonely stump throws a surprise dance,
With moths as partners, oh, what a chance!
The moss holds a party, all green and bright,
Where mushrooms wear hats and twirl in delight.

Rabbits in tuxedos take center stage,
With a tap dance routine, they break from the cage.
While beetles provide the music, sweet and funny,
In this silent grove, laughter flows like honey.

Yet shadows of pines can't help but grumble,
'It's a bit much, don't you think? We could tumble!'
But nature just smiles with a wink and a jig,
As echoes of laughter make everyone dig!

The Last Bloom of Memory

In the twilight where memories sway,
A last bloom chuckles, 'I'll save the day!'
With petals still bright, it holds a great show,
'See how I shine, even in woe!'

The bees remind it of youthful glee,
'You danced once, now you sip your tea!'
'I'll dance again, just wait for the sun!'
But forgetful petals just sigh, 'What fun!'

Old vases with cracks roll their eyes with sass,
'We keep your stories, but they've lost their class.'
A waltz of memories turns into jest,
In a world where blooms seek a funny fest.

With laughter and joy, they burst into bloom,
For even in fading, there's laughter to loom.
The last bloom of memory stands bold and high,
Creating a chuckle as the world bids goodbye!

The Last Blooming

In the garden of dreams, a sprout was seen,
Dancing with weeds, oh so carefree.
A flower so bright, with not much to show,
Claims it's the star of the seasonal show.

But pesky old daisies laugh in the sun,
'You think you're so grand, but we're just more fun!'
The petals all curl, the laughter gets loud,
As the last blooming tries to join the crowd.

Yet in this wild dance, a truth they can't hide,
Even the wilted can take the joyride.
With roots in the soil, they all agree,
In the garden of life, we're all quite the spree.

So next time you see one withering away,
Join the parade; let colors display.
For all those who wilt shall blossom again,
In the laughter of blooms and joy of the pen.

Serenade of the Withered

A tune from the stems, a melody sweet,
Withered leaves whistle, a quirky heartbeat.
They sing of the rain that forgot how to pour,
While cracking their jokes 'bout the garden's old lore.

'Hey look at us, we're all quite a sight!
Still cracking up under this pale moonlight!'
With twirls and confusion, they sway in the breeze,
The withered ones chuckle, they do it with ease.

Now blooms may be blooming, in colors so loud,
But the fun's in their stories, they draw quite the crowd.
'We've tangoed with drought, and danced with decay,
Yet here we are still, with music to play!'

So raise up your glass, to the leaves that have stayed,
In the shadows of life, their humor displayed.
For in every dry leaf, a tale to be spun,
The serenade's laughter has only begun.

Lament of the Silent Leaves

Silent leaves whisper, lamenting the breeze,
'Thought we'd be lively, but now we're at ease.
Gone are the rumbles of storms in our hair,
We're just quiet spectators in nature's grand fair.'

With colors so faded, they start to confide,
'We're not just old fogies; we've got the right pride!
While flowers may flutter and flaunt every hue,
We're the wise ones who've seen more than a few.'

So charmed by their stories that we almost forgot,
How laughter can blossom in every small spot.
With humor so dry, it's like wine in a barrel,
These silent leaves giggle, alive with great peril.

In their tales of neglect, there's a truth we behold,
It's not just the vibrant that can be bold.
For whispers and giggles can flourish and thrive,
If you look for the joy, you'll see it alive.

Beneath the Sage Sky

Beneath the sage sky, the giggles unfold,
A canvas of chaos, so funny, so bold.
The blossoms unite for a comical jest,
Dancing with breezes, together they're blessed.

A daisy, a marigold, banding as friends,
Rush in with a punchline; the laughter transcends.
'Why did the rose refuse to play tag?'
It sighed, 'Because I'm thorny, and that's quite a drag!'

With petals aglow, their secrets should show,
That humor can flourish, that much we all know.
So while sunshine may brighten the blooms every day,
It's giggles and grins that keep gloom far away.

So come, take a seat under skies painted gray,
Join the laughter and bloom in a witty ballet.
For life's all a stage, and each of us plays
We'll dance through the weeds in this humorous maze.

The Last Whisper of the Bloom

In the garden where shadows play,
The pruners dance, oh what a fray!
Petals flutter, a gossip spree,
'He pruned me wrong!' calls out the pea.

Dandelions laugh in the sun's bright beam,
'We're weeds, but we're living the dream!'
While pansies pout, so full of pride,
'Dandelions are just weeds on the slide!'

The roses sigh with their fragrant tales,
'Don't ask us how to dodge the snails.'
Bumblebees buzz with a cheeky grin,
'We've seen worse days; let the fun begin!'

At dusk they gather, a blooming crowd,
Telling tales, both funny and loud.
A garden's laugh, in petals bestowed,
Where each joke's a seed in laughter sowed.

Emblems of the Heart's Weeping

In a flower shop, where love's on sale,
A tulip winked, with a mischievous trail.
'I'm the heart's wish,' it teased with flair,
While violets snickered, 'Who needs repair?'

The sunflowers rolled their golden eyes,
'When asked out, we're the ones who rise!'
While lilies giggled, waltzing so sweet,
'Date a rose? That's a thorny feat!'

Cherries blushed in a fruity twist,
'We're the sweetest, so can't resist!'
But mint jumped in, fresh with a laugh,
'Love's a cocktail, let's sip the half!'

In this bouquet, where humor reigns,
Each petal whispers of love's silly gains.
A heart that blossoms, and yet it weeps,
In laughter's embrace, fun laughter keeps.

The Ghosts of Flora's Embrace

In the haunted garden, petals prance,
The ghosts of blooms hold a silly dance.
'Boo!' cries the daisy, with a giggle bright,
While the marigolds shiver out of fright.

A lilac sways, with a ghostly tone,
'We once were purple, now we moan!'
Petunias chuckle, as shadows loom,
'At least we're not stuck in someone's room!'

The thistles poke at the lavender's hair,
'We missed the party; was it a scare?'
While roses blush in the moonlit glow,
'Ghosts can't prance, but we steal the show!'

In this eerie stretch of fragrant light,
A spooky soiree brings fun to the night.
With petals flapping in playful jest,
These spirits bloom, at humor's behest.

Herbal Echoes of the Past

In the pantry of herbs, a tale unfolds,
With thyme and sage, their laughter bold.
'We're the flavor,' said basil with glee,
'Without us, you'd just have boiled peas!'

The dill cracked jokes, all green and spry,
'Cucumber's bland, but we make it fly!'
While tarragon sang, a spicy refrain,
'Herbs unite; don't you feel the gain?'

Oregano sighed, a wise little sage,
'In stews and brews, we take center stage.'
But parsley piped up from the corner near,
'Don't forget me, I'm pretty dear!'

In this kitchen whirls laughter and cheer,
With herbs that echo, keeping year after year.
Together they blend, a merry delight,
In fragrant whispers, the past takes flight.

The Solace of Scented Remembrance

In the garden, herbs do dance,
Twirling leaves, they love to prance.
With every sniff, a memory flies,
Of past mistakes and silly lies.

A pot of stew should smell divine,
But burnt again, it's just my sign.
Oh fragrant friend, you save my day,
From kitchen chaos, lead the way!

The secret's here, inside your green,
Even if the dish looks mean.
With every chop, a giggle grows,
As thyme and sage join in the rows.

So let's embrace what herb can bake,
A funny twist in every flake.
For laughter lives where scents collide,
In herbal cheer, we must abide!

An Aroma's Lament

In a world where herbs unite,
They argue here, they bicker slight.
Basil claims, he's got the flair,
While thyme just sighs and twirls in air.

Cilantro winks, he steals the show,
While rosemary just lurks below.
"Why do they hate my woody charm?"
She questions, holding her fresh arm.

With each debate, a scent escapes,
Garlic dances in funny shapes.
So when they fight, I take a seat,
And munch on bread, it's quite the treat!

In the end, it's all a joke,
A flavorful mix, a fragrant cloak.
So let them bicker, let them fuss,
Just pass the bread and join the bus!

Embracing the Faded Green

In the corner by the sun,
Faded leaves, all worn from fun.
Each sprig has tales of kitchen blunders,
Of burnt toast and silly wonders.

Oh wilted friend, you still bring cheer,
With every scent, you draw me near.
Let's make a brew, the colors fade,
But your spirit's here, never betrayed.

Green turned brown, but what a laugh,
Imperfect, yet my perfect half.
With every whiff, nostalgia's found,
In your fuzzy arms, sweet love abounds.

So here's to you, old trusty leaf,
For every blend and every grief.
You teach us well, though faded bright,
In memory's hug, we find delight!

Glimpses into the Herb's Heart

Peek inside, a leafy heart,
Where all the crazy flavors start.
Sage giggles, oregano grins,
They've seen the battles, they know the wins.

Amid the scents, a spice convention,
Herbs unite with great intention.
Lavender's calm, while mint's a joker,
Turning meals into silly poker.

"Let's add some zest!" the herbs all cry,
To coax the taste buds, oh my, oh my!
And when they blend, it's sheer delight,
Making every meal a funny flight.

So gather round, the herbs, they say,
Embrace the mess in a funny way.
For laughter lives in every bite,
In herb-filled hearts, we find our light!

www.ingramcontent.com/pod-product-compliance
Lightning Source LLC
Chambersburg PA
CBHW071824160426
43209CB00003B/202